The Backyard Wedding Planner

www.affordableweddingvenuesandmenus.com

Introduction

Congratulations on your engagement!

I'm so glad you picked up this book - you're probably planning a backyard wedding of your own. And you already know how great it's going to be. Having your wedding at home means you can:

- Style your wedding any way you want
- Stick to your budget
- Choose any vendor
- Avoid minimums, time limits and other restrictions
- Create a wedding that's completely personal and totally you!

Now all you need to do is plan it. You probably have some ideas already, about food and entertainment. But there's so many moving parts that it's gotten a bit confusing. There's so much to think about. Maybe you're already asking yourself: "How many people will fit in our yard? Do we really need a tent? How many dishes do we need? How much alcohol should we buy?"

And the biggest question of all:
"How will we organize all this?"

Maybe you've already tried a big binder or a generic planner but it's not really working for your wedding. The typical planner tries to cover all the possibilities so you end up with a bunch of stuff you don't need. Then, to make it worse - they stick to typical venues. So you're missing a lot of important things that you'll need for your backyard wedding. The Backyard Wedding Planner covers all the possibilities, too. But everything is tailored for having your wedding at home.

How to Use This Book:

- The planner is set up workbook style, to walk you through all the details. Just fill in the blanks and you'll have everything covered.
- There's a lot of suggestions for your wedding: lawn games, floor plans, food and drinks. But all of it is optional. Pick and choose which elements are important to you and concentrate on those.
- The planner has tons of space for notes. You'll have a place to keep all your research, plans and details organized.
- Most importantly: don't stress about the details too much. Of course you'll make things nice, but remember that this is just the beginning. The beginning of your life together, in your home, surrounded by family and friends. The memories you're making are more important than any detail, in any book or checklist.

Thanks for picking up this planner - I hope you have fun with it.
And I hope your wedding is everything you dream.
Happy Planning!

Planning Timeline

12 Months Before Your Wedding

- ❏ Celebrate your engagement!
- ❏ Decide on the style and formality of your wedding
- ❏ Set your budget
- ❏ Talk to family members who want to contribute
- ❏ Start thinking about your guest list
- ❏ Decide what kind of a ceremony you want
- ❏ Decide where to hold your wedding ceremony
- ❏ Determine that your backyard is the right size for your wedding plan
- ❏ Check with your city officials about noise, safety or parking bylaws
- ❏ Do a walkthrough of your property
- ❏ Create an action list and add those items to your calendar
- ❏ Choose your wedding date

11 Months Before Your Wedding

- ❏ If you need a venue for your ceremony, book it as soon as possible
- ❏ Book the officiant for your ceremony
- ❏ Research catering options & start planning your menu
- ❏ Book your rentals including tents, tables, chairs and dishes
- ❏ Make a weather plan, just in case
- ❏ Choose your wedding party and ask them

10 Months Before Your Wedding

- ❏ Book your caterer or work on a DIY schedule to prepare your food
- ❏ Order your wedding dress
- ❏ Choose and book your photographer
- ❏ Choose and book a DJ or band

9 Months Before Your Wedding

- ❏ Finalize your guest list
- ❏ Send your Save the Date cards

8 Months Before Your Wedding

- ❏ Choose the bridesmaid dresses and make sure they get ordered
- ❏ Decide if you need a florist and book one

7 Months Before Your Wedding

- ❏ Book a rehearsal dinner venue
- ❏ Start to plan extra events like showers, welcome parties, etc

6 Months Before Your Wedding
- ❏ Register for gifts
- ❏ Choose a baker for your wedding cake
- ❏ Start to book, buy or make your entertainment - yard games, photo booths, etc.

5 Months Before Your Wedding
- ❏ Book any transportation required
- ❏ Book your honeymoon
- ❏ If you need it for your honeymoon, make sure your passport is up to date
- ❏ Buy or rent the grooms outfit

4 Months Before Your Wedding
- ❏ Do any courses or counselling required for your ceremony
- ❏ Choose groomsmen outfits and make sure they get booked
- ❏ Attend a tasting with your caterer
- ❏ Choose your cake
- ❏ Book hair and makeup

3 Months Before Your Wedding
- ❏ Buy your wedding bands
- ❏ Order or make your invitations
- ❏ Schedule fittings for groom
- ❏ Hair and makeup trials
- ❏ Finalize your menu, either with caterer or your DIY plan
- ❏ Meet your officiant
- ❏ Write your vows
- ❏ Choose readings and music for the ceremony

2 Months Before Your Wedding
- ❏ Mail your invitations
- ❏ Send rehearsal dinner invitations
- ❏ Attend your first dress fitting
- ❏ Make sure the wedding party dresses and suits are on track
- ❏ Make or order favours for your guests

6 Weeks Before Your Wedding
- ❏ Attend your second dress fitting
- ❏ Does your wedding party have all their clothes, including accessories?
- ❏ Work on a seating chart
- ❏ Make or order escort cards and place cards

1 Month Before Your Wedding

- ❏ Get your marriage license
- ❏ RSVPs are due. Follow up with any not received
- ❏ Buy wedding party gifts
- ❏ Do a mock up of centrepieces and decorations
- ❏ Make a playlist for your reception or give your selections to your DJ
- ❏ Check on your vendor payment schedules
- ❏ Do a final walkthrough of your property
- ❏ Create your Day-of Timeline
- ❏ Make appointments for salon or spa treatments

2 Weeks Before Your Wedding

- ❏ Break in your wedding shoes
- ❏ Confirm time for any vendor deliveries - update your Day-of Timeline
- ❏ Make a packing list for your honeymoon

1 Week Before Your Wedding

- ❏ Final dress fitting
- ❏ Try on your entire ensemble
- ❏ Put cash in tip envelopes to be handed out day-of
- ❏ Write out checks if there are vendors to be paid on day-of
- ❏ Final head count - for whoever is preparing your food
- ❏ Share your Day-of Timeline with your helpers or co-ordinators
- ❏ Attend your salon or spa appointments

1 Day Before Your Wedding

- ❏ Rehearse your ceremony with your officiant and wedding party
- ❏ Hold your rehearsal dinner
- ❏ Hand out gifts
- ❏ Print out your vows

Day of Your Wedding

- ❏ Get Married!

After Your Wedding

- ❏ Return any rentals (clothes, decorations, etc)
- ❏ Make sure all your vendors have been paid
- ❏ Look at your wedding photos and choose your prints or albums
- ❏ Send thank you notes to all your guests

Congratulations!

Walkthrough Your Property

Now that your home is your wedding venue you'll need to look at it with an impartial eye. Pretend you're a guest arriving on the day of your wedding and give your property an honest look. Then decide how you'll make it as welcoming as possible. Don't worry about fancy landscaping if that's not in the cards for you right now. Welcoming means neat, tidy and well taken care of. Work with what you have to extend your hospitality and your guests will feel welcomed and loved.

Start at the front curb and take a look at your property:

Are the door and shutters freshly painted? _____

How does your mailbox look? _____

Is the grass neat and tidy? _____

Do you like your landscaping? _____

Are you planning to do any planting or gardening? _____

_____

_____

Where are your garbage and recycling bins? _____

Are your fences in good condition? _____

Are your sidewalks level and safe? _____

Are the patios, decks or porches easy to walk on? Are the handrails in good condition?

_____

_____

When your guests arrive:

Where will people park? _____

Is it obvious where to walk in? Will we need signs? _____

Where can people put their gifts? _____

Where should people sit or stand while they're waiting to start? _____

Is there shade? _____

If you're having your ceremony here:

Where will it happen? _____

Where will the officiant stand? _____

Is there space for an aisle? _____

Where will the wedding party walk to get to the officiant? _____

Where will the guests sit? _____

Is there noise that will interfere? Will you need a microphone and speaker? _____
_____

Will there be a receiving line after the ceremony? Where? _____
_____

If kids are invited:

Is there a separate play area for kids? _____

Are there any big things to child proof (like a pool, etc)? _____
_____

Is the yard enclosed? _____

Catering:

Where will the food service set up? _____

Is there enough space in the kitchen? _____

Is there enough power? _____

Consider your reception area:

Will there be mosquitos or bugs? Will you need coils or spray? Can you pre-plan
anything to keep the bug population down? _____
_____

If your reception is at night, how will you light it? _____

Is the house within extension cord distance or will you need a generator to get lights
and music to your ceremony or reception area? _____

If you're having 50 or more guests, is there space for a portable restroom? _____

If you're planning a bonfire

Check your local bylaws to make sure you're staying legal and safe: _____

Do you have a fire pit or will you build one? _____

What kind of seating will be around the fire? _____

Landscaping Projects

Name of Project: _____

Contractor: _____

Contact Name: _____

Contact Phone Number: _____

Project Includes: _____

_____

_____

_____

Date to Begin: _____

Completion Date: _____

Total Cost: _____

Deposit Paid: _____

Amount Due: _____

Notes: _____

_____

_____

◄ · ►

Name of Project: _____

Contractor: _____

Contact Name: _____

Contact Phone Number: _____

Project Includes: _____

_____

_____

_____

Date to Begin: _____

Completion Date: _____

Total Cost: _____

Deposit Paid: _____

Amount Due: _____

Notes: _____

_____

_____

Landscaping Projects

Name of Project: _____

Contractor: _____

Contact Name: _____

Contact Phone Number: _____

Project Includes: _____

_____

_____

_____

Date to Begin: _____

Completion Date: _____

Total Cost: _____

Deposit Paid: _____

Amount Due: _____

Notes: _____

_____

_____

◄ • ►

Name of Project: _____

Contractor: _____

Contact Name: _____

Contact Phone Number: _____

Project Includes: _____

_____

_____

_____

Date to Begin: _____

Completion Date: _____

Total Cost: _____

Deposit Paid: _____

Amount Due: _____

Notes: _____

_____

_____

Landscaping DIY

Name of Project: _____

Who's Doing It: _____

Tools & Materials: _____

_____

_____

_____

_____

_____

Cost: _____

Notes: _____

_____

_____

_____

Name of Project: _____

Who's Doing It: _____

Tools & Materials: _____

_____

_____

_____

_____

_____

Cost: _____

Notes: _____

_____

_____

_____

Landscaping DIY

Name of Project: _____

Who's Doing It: _____

Tools & Materials: _____

_____

_____

_____

_____

_____

Cost: _____

Notes: _____

_____

_____

_____

Name of Project: _____

Who's Doing It: _____

Tools & Materials: _____

_____

_____

_____

_____

_____

Cost: _____

Notes: _____

_____

_____

_____

Landscaping DIY

Name of Project: _____

Who's Doing It: _____

Tools & Materials: _____

_____

_____

_____

_____

_____

Cost: _____

Notes: _____

_____

_____

_____

Name of Project: _____

Who's Doing It: _____

Tools & Materials: _____

_____

_____

_____

_____

_____

Cost: _____

Notes: _____

_____

_____

_____

Creating a Floor Plan

You might have a huge yard, or you might have a tiny yard. Either way, a floor plan is a great way to start figuring out your wedding. Once you decide where everything goes you'll know exactly how much stuff to buy, borrow or rent. Use the graph paper on the next few pages to create your own floor plans.

Start by measuring out your yard and sketching in any permanent structures. Then decide where each event or activity is going to take place:

Events of the Day:
- Wedding Ceremony
- Receiving Line
- Cocktail Hour
- Reception
- Lawn Games
- Bonfire

The reception area will probably take the most finessing. This is where you'll start looking at table sizes and comparing it to your guest list.

In the reception area you might include:
- Tables & Chairs
- Head Table or Sweetheart Table
- Buffet Tables
- Cake Table
- Dessert Table
- Cookie Table
- Bar or Beverage Stand
- Guest Book Table
- Gift Table
- DJ or Music Table
- Dance Floor

The bigger things to consider:
- Tent (If you're getting a tent, remember to check how much space it needs - sometimes they need extra space for anchoring)
- Portable Restrooms
- Generator

Standard Table Sizes

Low Round Cocktail Tables - 30" Tall

- **30 inches**
- seats 3 or 4 guests for cocktails
- also used for sweetheart table or cake table
- order 90" round linen

- **3 feet** or 36 inches
- seats 4 guests for cocktails
- also used for sweetheart table or cake table
- order 96" round linen

High Round Cocktail Tables - 42" Tall

- **30 inches**
- standing rooms for cocktails
- order 108" round linen
- if you're tying a sash around the base, order 120" round linen

- **3 feet** or 36 inches
- standing room for cocktails
- order 120" round linen
- if you're tying a sash around the base, order 132" round linen

and Number of Seats

Round Tables

- **4 feet** or 48 inches
- used for sweetheart table or cake table
- order 108" round linen

- **5 feet** or 60 inches
- seats 8 guests
- order 120" round linen

- **6 feet** or 72 inches
- seats 10 guests
- order 132" round linen

Rectangle Tables

- **4 feet** long x 30" wide
- seats 4 guests
- also used as gift table, DJ table or buffet table
- order 90" x 108" linen

- **6 feet** long x 30" wide
- seats 6 guests
- also used as gift table, DJ table or buffet table
- order 90" x 132" linen

- **8 feet** long x 30" wide
- seats 8 guests
- also used as gift table, DJ table or buffet table
- order 90" x 156" linen

Weather Plan

It's tough to plan an outdoor wedding even a few months in advance. You just never know what the weather's going to do. You could get a heat wave, a cold front or just plain rain. Whatever happens, you need to be prepared. If you plan now, you won't need to panic at the last minute.

If you're lucky enough to have a barn or other structure, plan ahead in case you need to move the entire party indoors. If you don't have an indoor option, the best backup will be a tent. You could always reserve one and watch the weather forecasts. If you don't need it, you can cancel it a few weeks beforehand. Just make sure you understand the cancellation and refund policies when you sign the contract.

Most of your options will need advance reservations. So it's important to line it up as early as possible. Hopefully you won't need your backup weather plan. But if you do - you'll be so happy you have one!

If you don't have a barn or a tent, you can host inside:
- ❏ Your house
- ❏ A friend's house
- ❏ Park with a shelter
- ❏ Community center
- ❏ Church hall
- ❏ Restaurant

Where will the ceremony be if it needs to move indoors: _____
_____

Where will the reception be if it needs to move indoors: _____
_____

Do you know where to borrow, buy or rent:
- ❏ Tent with walls and a floor
- ❏ Portable fans
- ❏ Portable air conditioners
- ❏ Portable heaters
- ❏ Generators
- ❏ Extension Cords
- ❏ Umbrellas
- ❏ Rubber boots

Notes:

Budget
The Big Picture

Home Venue $_____

Ceremony $_____

Food $_____

Beverages $_____

Wedding Cake $_____

Photography $_____

Rentals $_____

Paper Stuff $_____

Clothes & Grooming $_____

Flowers $_____

Decorations $_____

Entertainment $_____

Parking $_____

Gifts $_____

Total $_____

Planned Budget $_____

Budget
The Breakdown

Home Venue:
_____ Wedding Insurance
_____ Extra Home Insurance
_____ Permits
_____ Landscaping Projects
_____ Subtotal

Ceremony:
_____ Venue
_____ Officiant
_____ Wedding Rings
_____ Marriage License
_____ Transportation to
Reception
_____ Subtotal

Food:
_____ Food
_____ Catering Staff
_____ Gratuities
_____ Subtotal

Beverages:
_____ Beverages
_____ Bartender
_____ Gratuities
_____ Subtotal

Wedding Cake:
_____ Cake
_____ Cake Knife & Server
_____ Subtotal

Photography:
_____ Photographer
_____ Videographer
_____ Photo Booth
_____ Subtotal

Rentals:
_____ Tent
_____ Tables
_____ Chairs
_____ Tablecloths
_____ Napkins
_____ Dishes
_____ Chair Covers
_____ Bar
_____ Dance Floor
_____ Speakers
_____ Microphone
_____ Lighting
_____ Washroom
_____ Subtotal

Invitations & Cards::

_____ Save the Dates
_____ Invitation Cards
_____ RSVP Cards
_____ Thank You cards
_____ Announcements
_____ Postage Stamps
_____ Programs
_____ Escort Cards
_____ Place Cards
_____ Menu Cards
_____ Guest Book
_____ Pen for Guest Book
_____ Subtotal

Clothes & Grooming

_____ Dress
_____ Shoes
_____ Veil & Headpiece
_____ Accessories
_____ Makeup
_____ Hair Styling
_____ Suit
_____ Shirt & Socks
_____ Shoes
_____ Accessories
_____ Hair Styling
_____ Subtotal

Flowers:

_____ Bridal Bouquet
_____ Bridesmaids Bouquets
_____ Grooms Boutonnière
_____ Groomsmen
Boutonnières
_____ Mom & Grandma
Corsages
_____ Dad & Grandpa
Boutonnières
_____ Flower Girl Baskets
_____ Ring Bearer Pillow
_____ Floral Centrepieces
_____ Floral Ceremony Decor
_____ Subtotal

Decorations:

_____ Aisle Decoration
_____ Altar Decoration
_____ Car Decoration
_____ Reception
Decoration
_____ Centrepieces
_____ Cake Table
Decoration
_____ Head Table
Decoration
_____ Signage
_____ Subtotal

Entertainment:

_____ Favours for Guests
_____ Backyard Games
_____ Photo Booth
_____ DJ
_____ Subtotal

Parking:

_____ Valet Service
_____ Shuttle
_____ Subtotal

Gifts:

_____ For Bridesmaids
_____ For Groomsmen
_____ For Parents
_____ To Each Other
_____ Subtotal

Rehearsal Dinner:

_____ Rehearsal Venue
_____ Officiant
_____ Dinner
_____ Subtotal

Honeymoon:

_____ Flights
_____ Hotels
_____ Sightseeing
_____ Transportation
_____ Subtotal

Other:

_____
_____
_____
_____
_____
_____
_____
_____
_____

Payment Schedule

Item or Service	Total Amount	Deposit Amount	Final Payment	Due Date

Notes

Notes

Invitations

Your backyard wedding can be any style or theme. It can be as casual or formal as you like - and you can serve any food you want. Which is great, but it's important to let your guests know so they can come prepared. If the ceremony requires standing on grass, people don't want to show up wearing stilettos.

The same idea for food. It's ok if you're serving cake & punch, just let them know ahead of time so they can eat before they arrive. Once they realize it's at your house they'll have even more questions. So the goal of your invitations is to let them know what to expect.

First of all, make sure you've got the basics: your names, date, time and place. Then you can add more details.

Most of your guests' questions will revolve around what to wear and what to eat. Here's how you can convey the information:

- The style of your invitations will give the first impression. Do you want it to appear formal or casual?
- You can invite them to a garden ceremony, an outdoor ceremony or a backyard bash. Whichever goes with your style.
- The time of your wedding will let them know what to expect for food. When you're choosing the time, remember that if you invite people at dinner time - they need to be fed dinner.
- Come right out and say what you'll be serving. You can say "cake & punch reception to follow". Or "down home bbq, drinks and dancing".

You want your guests to get excited about your wedding, so go ahead and get creative. Just remember that this is the info your guests will be using to prepare. So be as clear as you can about what you're inviting them to.

Guest List

Notes

The Ceremony

Location: _____

Time: _____

Officiant: _____

Prelude Music: _____

Honoured Guests are seated: _____
_____

Processional Music: _____

Processional: _____

Officiant's Opening Remarks

Vows

Exchange of Rings

Unity Ceremony: _____
_____
_____

Traditions: _____
_____
_____

Pronouncement

The Kiss

Recessional Music: _____

Recessional

Notes: _____
_____
_____
_____
_____
_____
_____

Notes

Figuring Out the Food

One of the greatest things about your backyard wedding is that you can serve any food you want. You can have traditional catering or you can order from a restaurant. You can get food trucks to come over. If you want to, you can have a potluck dinner. Or have your local church ladies make a home cooked meal for your guests. If you're really ambitious you can even make the food yourself.

When you're thinking about what to serve, consider:
- How long do you want your wedding to be?
- The more food there is, the longer people will stay.
- You can do cake and punch, or a cocktail party with appetizers. Just don't expect people to stay and dance all night unless you've got enough food to fuel them.
- If you invite people at a meal time, you need to feed them a meal. If you invite people at dinner time, and give them nothing but cake they'll leave pretty quickly - to go get dinner!

If you're thinking about doing DIY for your food:
- How complicated is your menu?
- Do you have experience cooking for large groups?
- Keep in mind all the extra chores that go with catering - serving, cleaning, etc.
- Remember, if you're planning to have your family or friends organize and serve the food, accept that they'll be working at your wedding. There's nothing wrong with them helping - just be realistic about the fact that they'll have less time to eat, socialize and dance.

If you want an alternative to a sit down dinner, try a:
- ❏ Breakfast Wedding
- ❏ Brunch Wedding
- ❏ Wedding Luncheon
- ❏ Cake and Punch Reception
- ❏ Tea Sandwiches and Desserts
- ❏ Cocktail Party

Questions for Potential Caterer #1

Business Name: _____

Contact Name and Number: _____

Can you cater an outdoor wedding, at a family home? _____

Are you licensed, with health permits and liability insurance? _____

Is a special event permit required for my reception? If so, will you handle getting it? __
_____

What are your minimums? Is it a certain price or number of guests? _____
_____

What's the range of prices for a per person meal package? _____
_____

What's included in the package (appetizers, dessert, coffee & tea, etc)? _____
_____
_____
_____

Food Preparation

Will the food be prepared on site or brought in already prepared? _____
_____

What will you need for water, equipment and electricity? _____
_____
_____

How long do you need to set up and break down the service? _____
_____

Dishes, Tables & Chairs

Can your staff handle place settings, centrepieces, place cards or favours? _____
_____

What kind of linens, glassware, china and cutlery can you provide? _____
_____

Can you handle table and chair rentals as well? _____
_____

The Staff On Site

What's the ratio of servers to guests? _____

What will the staff be wearing? _____

Is there an overtime charge if my reception goes long? _____

Serving Drinks

Do you offer bar packages? _____

Could you provide a bartender if we provide the alcohol? _____

Is there a corkage fee to serve wine at dinner? _____

Wedding Cake

If we serve wedding cake, is there a cake cutting fee? _____

Can you package the leftover cake and the top layer? _____

Special Requests

Can you accommodate allergies or restrictions? _____

How much do you charge for vendor meals? _____

How much do you charge for kids meals? _____

Booking Your Service

Do you provide menu tastings? Is ther
charge? _____
_____

When do I need to sign the contract?
_____

What's the minimum deposit required
_____
_____

What's the cancellation or refund
policy?
_____
_____

When do you need the final guest
count?
_____

Questions for
Potential Caterer #2

Business Name: _____

Contact Name and Number: _____

Can you cater an outdoor wedding, at a family home? _____

Are you licensed, with health permits and liability insurance? _____

Is a special event permit required for my reception? If so, will you handle getting it? __
_____

What are your minimums? Is it a certain price or number of guests? _____
_____

What's the range of prices for a per person meal package? _____
_____

What's included in the package (appetizers, dessert, coffee & tea, etc)? _____
_____
_____
_____

Food Preparation

Will the food be prepared on site or brought in already prepared? _____
_____

What will you need for water, equipment and electricity? _____
_____
_____

How long do you need to set up and break down the service? _____
_____

Dishes, Tables & Chairs

Can your staff handle place settings, centrepieces, place cards or favours? _____
_____

What kind of linens, glassware, china and cutlery can you provide? _____
_____

Can you handle table and chair rentals as well? _____
_____

The Staff On Site

What's the ratio of servers to guests? _____

What will the staff be wearing? _____

Is there an overtime charge if my reception goes long? _____

Serving Drinks

Do you offer bar packages? _____

Could you provide a bartender if we provide the alcohol? _____

Is there a corkage fee to serve wine at dinner? _____

Wedding Cake

If we serve wedding cake, is there a cake cutting fee? _____

Can you package the leftover cake and the top layer? _____

Special Requests

Can you accommodate allergies or restrictions? _____

How much do you charge for vendor meals? _____

How much do you charge for kids meals? _____

Booking Your Service

Do you provide menu tastings? Is ther charge? _____
_____

When do I need to sign the contract?
_____

What's the minimum deposit required
_____
_____

What's the cancellation or refund policy?
_____
_____
_____

When do you need the final guest count?
_____

Questions for
Potential Caterer #3

Business Name: _____

Contact Name and Number: _____

Can you cater an outdoor wedding, at a family home? _____

Are you licensed, with health permits and liability insurance? _____

Is a special event permit required for my reception? If so, will you handle getting it? __

_____

What are your minimums? Is it a certain price or number of guests? _____

_____

What's the range of prices for a per person meal package? _____

_____

What's included in the package (appetizers, dessert, coffee & tea, etc)? _____

_____

_____

_____

Food Preparation

Will the food be prepared on site or brought in already prepared? _____

_____

What will you need for water, equipment and electricity? _____

_____

_____

How long do you need to set up and break down the service? _____

_____

Dishes, Tables & Chairs

Can your staff handle place settings, centrepieces, place cards or favours? _____

_____

What kind of linens, glassware, china and cutlery can you provide? _____

_____

Can you handle table and chair rentals as well? _____

_____

The Staff On Site

What's the ratio of servers to guests? _____

What will the staff be wearing? _____

Is there an overtime charge if my reception goes long? _____

Serving Drinks

Do you offer bar packages? _____

Could you provide a bartender if we provide the alcohol? _____

Is there a corkage fee to serve wine at dinner? _____

Wedding Cake

If we serve wedding cake, is there a cake cutting fee? _____

Can you package the leftover cake and the top layer? _____

Special Requests

Can you accommodate allergies or restrictions? _____

How much do you charge for vendor meals? _____

How much do you charge for kids meals? _____

Booking Your Service

Do you provide menu tastings? Is ther
charge? _____

_____

When do I need to sign the contract?

_____

What's the minimum deposit required

_____

_____

What's the cancellation or refund
policy?

_____

_____

_____

When do you need the final guest
count?

_____

Restaurant Catering

If you want to save a ton of money you can order food from your favourite restaurant. Most restaurants can provide food for a large number of people. The major difference from a full service caterer is that you'll need to figure out how to serve it yourself. Even if you hire help to get the food warmed up and onto the tables you can still save a lot of money. Plus, you'll have more freedom over the food you serve. You can choose your favourite dishes from a great restaurant without worrying about a pre-packaged menu.

Questions to ask Restaurant #1

Restaurant Name: _____

Contact Name and Number: _____

Will you deliver the food hot or will it need to be heated up? _____
_____

Will it be served buffet style or family style? _____

What kind of containers will it be delivered in? _____

Will you set up the food, chafing dishes, etc? _____

Can you provide staff to serve and clean up? _____

Can you provide a bartender? _____

What date do I need to reserve by? _____

Do you need a deposit? _____

What if I need to cancel? _____

Notes: _____
_____
_____

Questions to ask Restaurant #2

Restaurant Name: _____

Contact Name and Number: _____

Will you deliver the food hot or will it need to be heated up? _____

_____

Will it be served buffet style or family style? _____

What kind of containers will it be delivered in? _____

Will you set up the food, chafing dishes, etc? _____

Can you provide staff to serve and clean up? _____

Can you provide a bartender? _____

What date do I need to reserve by? _____

Do you need a deposit? _____

What if I need to cancel? _____

Notes: _____

_____

_____

Questions to ask yourself:

Who will warm up the food and set it out? _____

_____

_____

Who will serve or keep the buffet table clean and stocked? _____

_____

_____

Who will clean up and put away leftovers? _____

_____

_____

Who will wash the serving pieces? _____

_____

_____

Who will take away the trash? _____

_____

Planning a Potluck

Nothing starts controversy like mentioning a potluck wedding! But lots of people do it and it's totally ok. In fact - it's better than ok. Potluck weddings are friendly and fun. Sharing food brings people together and builds community. There's nothing better than celebrating your wedding with a meal cooked by your loved ones. If you plan carefully, your potluck wedding will be a huge success.

Will Potluck Work For Your Wedding?

Are you the right couple for a potluck wedding?

The more contributions other people make, the less control you'll have. Are you ok not being in charge of every detail? _____

You'll need to provide some dishes to anchor or fill out the meal. What will you be providing?

_____
_____
_____

Most couples ask for potluck food in lieu of gifts. Are you ok with less gifts? _____
_____
_____

Do you have the right guests?

Are your guests mostly local? (It's tough to travel with a dish for potluck) _____
_____

Does your community regularly do church or party potlucks? _____
_____

Are your guests people who cook? Some people just aren't good at it. Is it ok if they bring store bought food? _____
_____

How many guests are coming? (The more guests, the more organized you'll need to be)
_____
_____

Do you have the space?

Where will you store the food you're providing? _____

Will people bring their dishes ahead of time? Or when they arrive? _____
_____

Where will the contributions be stored? _____

How much food will need to be reheated? Can your kitchen handle it? _____
_____

Do you have the help?

How will the food get from the kitchen to the table? _____
_____

Do you have church ladies or kitchen ladies who can help? _____
_____

Is there anyone you can hire to do the work of serving and cleaning up? _____
_____
_____

Tips:

- Think about the amount of food people will be bringing. It all needs to go somewhere while they have cocktails, mingle and socialize. It's unlikely people will start to eat as soon as they arrive and the food can't be sitting out for hours.
- **Be very careful about food safety: hot food must be kept hot and cold food must be kept cold.**
- Set up a Google spreadsheet where people can sign up for dishes to bring. You can put the link to it on your wedding webpage
- Prepare the table ahead of time with serving pieces, chafing dishes, etc. When it's time to serve, it'll be easier to place all the food and be ready to start dinner.
- If you can, hand out disposable aluminum trays to guests beforehand. If they use the right sizes for your chafing dishes, they can just be dropped in when it's time to serve dinner. And no worries about washing and returning casserole dishes.

Menu Ideas

Handling the Beverages

If you're using a caterer, they may be able to provide you with a bar package. If you don't have a caterer or want to save money, the bar is a great place to DIY. You can configure your bar any way you'd like. You can do anything from non alcoholic punch all the way to a full bar. You could do wine and beer or signature cocktails. Once you decide what to serve, you just need to do a bit of math and figure out how much to buy.

How Much Alcohol Will You Need?
To figure out how many drinks you'll need for your reception first consider your guest list, then do a bit of math. Figure out the averages first, then adjust for your crowds drinking habits.

Start by multiplying your number of guests by the number of hours for your reception. Then allow 1 drink per hour

Example: 150 guests x 3 hours = 450 drinks
If you're serving only wine and beer, it's usually split 60/40
From the example:
60% of 450 drinks = 270 glasses of wine
40% of 450 drinks = 180 beers

If you'll be offering mixed drinks or cocktails as well as beer and wine, the ratio becomes
50% wine, 20% beer, 30% liquor
50% of 450 drinks = 225 glasses of wine
20% of 450 drinks = 90 beers
30% of 450 drinks = 135 mixed drinks

How Much in a Bottle?
A bottle of wine 750mL = 5 glasses of wine
A bottle of champagne 750 mL = 6 to 8 glasses of champagne
A keg of beer = 165 beers (12 oz each)
A bottle of spirits 750mL = 12 mixed drinks

Non-alcoholic
Remember to account for non-drinkers or kids who'll be at your reception and have some juice or soft drinks available

Doing the Math:

of Guests _____ x # of hours _____

= # of Drinks _____

Notes

Beverages Checklist

You don't need everything on the list - pick and choose what you'll want for favourite drinks or what you'll need to create your signature cocktails:

- ❏ Champagne or Sparkling Wine
- ❏ Red Wine
- ❏ White Wine
- ❏ Beer

- ❏ Bourbon
- ❏ Rum
- ❏ Gin
- ❏ Scotch
- ❏ Tequila
- ❏ Vodka
- ❏ Brandy
- ❏ Whiskey

- ❏ Oranges
- ❏ Lemons
- ❏ Limes
- ❏ Cherries
- ❏ Pineapple
- ❏ Olives
- ❏ Cocktail Onions

- ❏ Water
- ❏ Tonic
- ❏ Club Soda
- ❏ Cola & Diet Cola
- ❏ Lemon Lime & Diet Lemon Lime
- ❏ Orange Juice
- ❏ Cranberry Juice
- ❏ Tomato Juice
- ❏ Lemonade
- ❏ Iced Tea
- ❏ Coffee & Tea

- ❏ Ice

Notes

Wedding Cake

The most popular way to end your dinner is with a wedding cake. The cake is such an important part of a wedding that it's considered rude to leave before it's been cut and served. There are lots of other options, but if you want to please your guests and have a great photo opp at the same time - nothing beats a beautiful cake.

When you're choosing your cake, keep in mind that buttercream icing will sweat and melt as soon as it gets hot. A fondant cake can stand up to the heat better, but any cake should be kept cool and out of the sun. Make sure your baker knows your wedding is outdoors and ask for their advice.

If you've got a caterer they might want you to purchase your cake through them. If they've got good reviews and you're happy with the cakes they offer, this could be your easiest choice. If you've got your own baker the caterer might charge you a cutting fee - usually $1.50 to $2.00 a slice.

The Baker's Contract Should Include:
- Date, time and location for delivery
- Total price of the cake, including delivery fees
- Deposit paid
- Amount due and date to be paid
- A written description that lists the type of icing, decoration, cake, filling and the number of servings
- Any flowers or topper that will be provided b

Questions for Your Baker:

How far ahead is the cake baked? _____

_____

Do you use frozen cakes? _____

_____

How much is the delivery charge? _____

_____

Will you provide the topper or flowers? _____

_____

Is a deposit required? _____

_____

When is the final payment due? _____

_____

Rental Worksheets

It looks like there's a lot on these sheets - and there is! But don't panic. It includes every single thing you can think of and you probably won't need all of it. The next few pages list everything from the tent to salt & pepper shakers. So take your time going through it and decide what you'll actually need to get. You can also check with your caterer. Sometimes they'll handle all the rentals including dishes and linens.

If you sketched out your floor plan earlier you can transfer the number of tables and chairs straight into these worksheets, then start looking up prices and calling for quotes.

Remember to ask your rental provider:

Is there a delivery fee? _____

Is there a minimum order? _____

How long does it take to set up? _____
_____

When do I need to finalize my order numbers? _____

What is the cancellation and refund policy? _____
_____

Reception Tent

Number of Guests: _____

Tent Size: _____

Price for Tent: _____

Price for Walls: _____

Price for Tent Floor: _____

Total: _____

Tent Accessories

Dance Floor: _____

Bar: _____

Lighting: _____

Electric Fans: _____

Portable Heaters: _____

Microphones: _____

Speakers: : _____

Generator: _____

Trash Cans: _____

Total: _____

Dinner & Cocktail Tables

Rectangle Tables

8 Foot Tables #_____ x Price per Table $_____ = $_____

6 Foot Tables #_____ x Price per Table $_____ = $_____

4 Foot Tables #_____ x Price per Table $_____ = $_____

Round Tables

6 Foot Tables #_____ x Price per Table $_____ = $_____

5 Foot Tables #_____ x Price per Table $_____ = $_____

4 Foot Tables #_____ x Price per Table $_____ = $_____

3 Foot Tables #_____ x Price per Table $_____ = $_____

30 Inch Tables #_____ x Price per Table $_____ = $_____

Tall Round Tables

3 Foot Tables #_____ x Price per Table $_____ = $_____

30 Inch Tables #_____ x Price per Table $_____ = $_____

Total: _____

Additional Tables

Food Tables: Shape & Size _____ Table Price $ _____

Guest Book Table: Shape & Size _____ Table Price $ _____

Cake Table: Shape & Size _____ Table Price $ _____

Gift Table: Shape & Size _____ Table Price $ _____

Dessert Table: Shape & Size _____ Table Price $ _____

DJ or Music Table: Shape & Size _____ Table Price $ _____

Total: _____

Seating

Number of Chairs for Ceremony _____ x Price per Chair $_____ = $_____

Number of Chairs for Reception _____ x Price per Chair $_____ = $_____

Number of Chair Covers _____ x Price per Cover $_____ = $_____

Number of Chair Sashes _____ x Price per Sash $_____ = $_____

Total: _____

Dinner & Cocktail Linens

Rectangle Table Linens

8 Foot Linens #_____ x Price per Cloth $_____ = $_____

    Overlays #_____ x Price per Piece $_____ = $_____

6 Foot Linens #_____ x Price per Cloth $_____ = $_____

    Overlays #_____ x Price per Piece $_____ = $_____

4 Foot Linens #_____ x Price per Cloth $_____ = $_____

    Overlays #_____ x Price per Piece $_____ = $_____

Round Table Linens

6 Foot Linens #_____ x Price per Cloth $_____ = $_____

    Overlays #_____ x Price per Piece $_____ =$_____

5 Foot Linens #_____ x Price per Cloth $_____ =$_____

    Overlays #_____ x Price per Piece $_____ =$_____

4 Foot Linens #_____ x Price per Cloth $_____ =$_____

    Overlays #_____ x Price per Piece $_____ =$_____

3 Foot Linens #_____ x Price per Cloth $_____ =$_____

    Overlays #_____ x Price per Piece $_____ =$_____

30 Inch Linens #_____ x Price per Cloth $_____ =$_____

    Overlays #_____ x Price per Piece $_____ =$_____

Tall Round Table Linens

3 Foot Linens #_____ x Price per Cloth $_____ =$_____

    Overlays #_____ x Price per Piece $_____ = $_____

30 Inch Linens #_____ x Price per Cloth $_____ = $_____

    Overlays #_____ x Price per Piece $_____ = $_____

Napkins #_____ x Price per Napkin $_____ = $_____

Total: _____

Additional Table Linens

Food Tables: Shape & Size _____ Linen Price $ _____

Guest Book Table: Shape & Size _____ Linen Price $ _____

Cake Table: Shape & Size _____ Linen Price $ _____

Gift Table: Shape & Size _____ Linen Price $ _____

Dessert Table: Shape & Size _____ Linen Price $ _____

DJ or Music Table: Shape & Size _____ Linen Price $ _____

Total: _____

Additional Rentals

_____

_____

_____

_____

_____

_____

_____

_____

_____

Total: _____

Grand Total: _____

Notes

Renting Dishes

Ordering the right amount of dishes for your wedding is part science and part guesswork. If you can, let your caterer handle the rentals for you. All you'll need to do is give them your number of guests and they'll do all the rest. If you want to do the ordering yourself, here's some general guidelines:

For a Cocktail Party:

- Order 3 appetizer plates per person

For a Sit Down Dinner:

- Order the exact number of china dishes, flatware and water glasses + an extra 20% (to account for extra guests and breakage)

For a Buffet Dinner:

- Order 2 appetizer plates per person
- 2.5 dinner plates per person
- 2 dinner forks & knives per person
- 1.5 soup spoons per person
- 1.5 dessert forks per person
- Exact number of teaspoons

How Much Glassware To Order:

- Multiply the number of guests by the number of hours and allow 1 drink per hour
- Example: 150 guests x 3 hours = 450 drinks
- If you're serving only wine and beer, it's usually split 60/40
- From the example:
  - 60% of 450 drinks = 270 wine glasses;
  - 40% of 450 drinks = 180 beer glasses
- If you're having a sit down dinner, add another wine glass per person for the table setting
- If you'll be offering mixed drinks or cocktails as well as beer and wine, the ratio becomes 50% wine, 20% beer, 30% liquor

Dinnerware & Glassware

China

Appetizer Plates #_____ x Price per Piece $_____ = $_____

Charger Plates #_____ x Price per Piece $_____ = $_____

Salad Plates #_____ x Price per Piece $_____ = $_____

Soup Bowls #_____ x Price per Piece $_____ = $_____

Bread Plates #_____ x Price per Piece $_____ = $_____

Dinner Plates #_____ x Price per Piece $_____ = $_____

Cake Plates #_____ x Price per Piece $_____ = $_____

Cup & Saucer #_____ x Price per Piece $_____ = $_____

Total: _____

Cutlery

Salad Forks #_____ x Price per Piece $_____ = $_____

Soup Spoons #_____ x Price per Piece $_____ = $_____

Dinner Forks #_____ x Price per Piece $_____ = $_____

Butter Knives #_____ x Price per Piece $_____ = $_____

Steak Knives #_____ x Price per Piece $_____ = $_____

Cake Forks #_____ x Price per Piece $_____ = $_____

Teaspoons #_____ x Price per Piece $_____ = $_____

Total: _____

Glassware

Water Glasses #_____ x Price per Piece $_____ = $_____

Wine Glasses #_____ x Price per Piece $_____ = $_____

Beer Glasses #_____ x Price per Piece $_____ = $_____

Champagne
Flutes #_____ x Price per Piece $_____ = $_____

Multipurpose
Glasses #_____ x Price per Piece $_____ = $_____

Martini Glasses #_____ x Price per Piece $_____ = $_____

Total: _____

Dinner Service Pieces

Serving Dishes

Serving Bowls   #_____ x Price per Piece $_____   = $_____

Serving Platters #_____ x Price per Piece $_____   = $_____

Chafing Dishes   #_____ x Price per Piece $_____   = $_____

Punch Bowls   #_____ x Price per Piece $_____   = $_____

Coffee Urns   #_____ x Price per Piece $_____   = $_____

Tea Pots   #_____ x Price per Piece $_____   = $_____

Water Pitchers   #_____ x Price per Piece $_____   = $_____

Total: _____

Cutlery

Serving Forks   #_____ x Price per Piece $_____   = $_____

Serving Spoons   #_____ x Price per Piece $_____   = $_____

Salad Tongs   #_____ x Price per Piece $_____   = $_____

Soup Ladle   #_____ x Price per Piece $_____   = $_____

Gravy Ladle   #_____ x Price per Piece $_____   = $_____

Punch Ladle   #_____ x Price per Piece $_____   = $_____

Dessert Tongs   #_____ x Price per Piece $_____   = $_____

Total: _____

Accessories

Bread Baskets   #_____ x Price per Piece $_____   = $_____

Table Signs   #_____ x Price per Piece $_____   = $_____

Bottle Opener   #_____ x Price per Piece $_____   = $_____

Martini Shaker   #_____ x Price per Piece $_____   = $_____

Salt & Pepper   #_____ x Price per Piece $_____   = $_____

Cream & Sugar   #_____ x Price per Piece $_____   = $_____

Total: _____

Grand Total: _____

Getting Dressed

There are so many places to get your wedding dress, you don't need to go to a full service salon if that's not your style. If you want the experience you should definitely spend a day trying on dresses. Once you know what style you're after you can check out:

- Department stores
- Consignment shops
- Chain salons (like David's)
- Retailers that have bridal selections (Anthropologie, J. Crew)
- Literally any store that carries dresses (Remember: you can wear any dress you're comfortable in)

If you do order your dress (or your bridesmaid dresses) from a salon you'll get a contract when you put down the deposit. It should include:

- Description of your dress or dresses
- The designer name, style number, fabric, size and colour
- Deposit amounts
- The remaining amount and the date it's due
- Alteration fees
- Number of fittings
- Cancellation and refund policies

Shopping List

For the Bride:
- ❑ Dress
- ❑ Veil or Headpiece
- ❑ Undergarments
- ❑ Jewellery
- ❑ Shoes

For the Groom:
- ❑ Suit
- ❑ Shirt
- ❑ Cufflinks
- ❑ Accessories
- ❑ Socks
- ❑ Shoes

For the Bridesmaids:
- ❑ Dresses
- ❑ Accessories
- ❑ Undergarments
- ❑ Jewellery
- ❑ Shoes

For the Groomsmen:
- ❑ Suit
- ❑ Shirt
- ❑ Cufflinks
- ❑ Accessories
- ❑ Socks
- ❑ Shoes

For the Flower Girl
- ❑ Dress
- ❑ Shoes
- ❑ Accessories

For the Ring Bearer
- ❑ Suit
- ❑ Shoes
- ❑ Accessories

To-Do List

- ❑ Ordered the dress
- ❑ Deposit paid $ _____
- ❑ Date dress is arriving: _____
- ❑ First Fitting Appointment: _____
- ❑ Second Fitting Appointment: _____
- ❑ Final Fitting Appointment: _____

- ❑ Measurements taken - ordered the suit
- ❑ Deposit paid $_____
- ❑ Date for Fitting and Pick up: _____

- ❑ Ordered dresses
- ❑ Deposits paid $_____
- ❑ Date dresses arriving: _____
- ❑ First fitting appointment: _____
- ❑ Final fitting appointment: _____

- ❑ Measurements taken - ordered the suits
- ❑ Deposit paid $_____
- ❑ Date for Fitting and Pick Up: _____

Other:
- ❑ _____
- ❑ _____
- ❑ _____
- ❑ _____
- ❑ _____
- ❑ _____

Notes

Photographer

Choosing your photographer

First, decide on the style you want. Every photographer has a different style and you should love the one you choose. Secondly, make sure you like the person. You'll be spending your entire wedding day together, so it should be someone you feel good with.

Third, spend some time talking with the photographer. Ask the following questions to make sure you've got all the info:

Potential Photographer #1

Is my wedding date available? _____

Have you done any weddings similar to ours? Have you shot an entire wedding outdoors before? _____

Can we give you a list of certain, specific photos we'd like? _____

Will you have an assistant with you? _____

If you're sick or unable to shoot our wedding, what's your backup plan for the day? ____ _____ _____

What time will you arrive? How long will you stay? _____ _____

If it goes over, can you stay longer? What is the overtime charge? _____ _____

What's the price range for packages? _____

What's included in the package? _____ _____ _____ _____

Do you edit and retouch the photos? _____

How long after the wedding will we see the photos? _____

Will you give us the digital negatives so we can print them ourselves? _____

What rights do we have to the images? Can we share them online? _____ _____

How much and when is the deposit required? _____

When is the final payment due?_____

What is your cancellation and refund policy? _____ _____

Potential Photographer #2

Is my wedding date available? _____

Have you done any weddings similar to ours? Have you shot an entire wedding outdoors before? _____

Can we give you a list of certain, specific photos we'd like? _____

Will you have an assistant with you? _____

If you're sick or unable to shoot our wedding, what's your backup plan for the day? _____
_____
_____

What time will you arrive? How long will you stay? _____
_____

If it goes over, can you stay longer? What is the overtime charge? _____
_____

What's the price range for packages? _____

What's included in the package? _____
_____
_____
_____
_____
_____

Do you edit and retouch the photos? _____

How long after the wedding will we see the photos? _____
_____

Will you give us the digital negatives so we can print them ourselves? _____
_____

What rights do we have to the images? Can we share them online? _____
_____
_____

How much and when is the deposit required? _____

When is the final payment due?_____

What is your cancellation and refund policy? _____
_____
_____

Potential Photographer #3

Is my wedding date available? _____

Have you done any weddings similar to ours? Have you shot an entire wedding outdoors before? _____

Can we give you a list of certain, specific photos we'd like? _____

Will you have an assistant with you? _____

If you're sick or unable to shoot our wedding, what's your backup plan for the day? _____
_____
_____

What time will you arrive? How long will you stay? _____
_____

If it goes over, can you stay longer? What is the overtime charge? _____
_____

What's the price range for packages? _____

What's included in the package? _____
_____
_____
_____
_____
_____

Do you edit and retouch the photos? _____

How long after the wedding will we see the photos? _____
_____

Will you give us the digital negatives so we can print them ourselves? _____
_____

What rights do we have to the images? Can we share them online? _____
_____
_____

How much and when is the deposit required? _____

When is the final payment due?_____

What is your cancellation and refund policy? _____
_____
_____

Notes

Decorations

Since you're having your wedding outdoors, rustic decor is a natural look for it. If that's what you want, go all out on the mason jars!

But don't think it's your only option. If you want your wedding to have a more elegant style it's easy enough to change the look with your decorations. Choose white for your linens and add breezy chiffon, fairy lights and lots of sparkling glass.

Whatever your style is, keep it in mind when you start choosing the decor for your ceremony and reception and you can get any look you want for your wedding.

There's a lot of options for finding your decorations. You can have a florist take care of it, or shop for them yourself. You can buy, borrow or rent stuff. You can look online or in local papers for brides who are selling supplies from their own weddings. Or head straight to Ikea or the dollar store. Just keep your style in mind while you look around at what's available. You might look for:

Mason Jars
Lanterns
Hurricane Glasses
Fairy Lights

Patio Lanterns
Mason Jars
Picnic Blankets
Wicker Baskets

Mirrors
Vases
River Stones
Glass Beads

Fabric
Ribbons
Bows

Glass Pitchers
Fish Bowls

Notes

Flowers

Ceremony:
- ❏ Bridal Bouquet
- ❏ Bridesmaids Bouquets
- ❏ Grooms Boutonnière
- ❏ Groomsmen Boutonnières
- ❏ Mom & Grandma Corsages
- ❏ Dad & Grandpa Boutonnières
- ❏ Flower Girl Baskets
- ❏ Aisle Decoration
- ❏ Altar Decoration

Reception:
- ❏ Centerpieces
- ❏ Cake Table Decor
- ❏ Gift Table Decor
- ❏ Guest Book Table Decor
- ❏ Tent Decoration

Questions to ask your florist:

Is our wedding date available? _____

Do you have a minimum order requirement? _____
_____

Can I review your portfolio? _____
_____

What flowers are in season on our wedding date? _____
_____
_____

What flowers would you recommend, based on our
colours and budget? _____
_____
_____

If I give you a picture I like can you recreate it? _____
_____

Is there a delivery fee? _____

How much time do you need to set up? _____
_____

Can you move the flowers from the ceremony to the
reception? _____

What is your cancellation and refund policy? _____
_____
_____

Notes

Entertainment

During your reception, there's always two great ways to entertain your guests:
- Music and Dancing
- Photo Booth

Since your wedding is outdoors, why not add a few lawn games for fun:
- Giant Jenga
- Cornhole
- Croquet
- Bocce ball
- Horseshoes
- Connect Four
- Ring Toss
- Ladder Golf
- Badminton
- Giant Tic Tac Toe
- Piñata
- Hula Hoops

While your guests are being entertained, consider providing a few things for their comfort. If you've got the budget it's always nice to add little extras:
- Bug spray
- Sunscreen
- Umbrellas
- Flip flops
- Pashminas
- Sunglasses

Notes

DIY Projects

Name of Project: _____

Who's Doing It: _____

Tools & Materials: _____

_____

_____

_____

_____

_____

Cost: _____

Notes: _____

_____

_____

_____

Name of Project: _____

Who's Doing It: _____

Tools & Materials: _____

_____

_____

_____

_____

_____

Cost: _____

Notes: _____

_____

_____

_____

DIY Projects

Name of Project: _____

Who's Doing It: _____

Tools & Materials: _____

_____

_____

_____

_____

_____

Cost: _____

Notes: _____

_____

_____

_____

Name of Project: _____

Who's Doing It: _____

Tools & Materials: _____

_____

_____

_____

_____

_____

Cost: _____

Notes: _____

_____

_____

_____

DIY Projects

Name of Project: _____

Who's Doing It: _____

Tools & Materials: _____

_____

_____

_____

_____

_____

_____

Cost: _____

Notes: _____

_____

_____

_____

Name of Project: _____

Who's Doing It: _____

Tools & Materials: _____

_____

_____

_____

_____

_____

_____

Cost: _____

Notes: _____

_____

_____

_____

DIY Projects

Name of Project: _____

Who's Doing It: _____

Tools & Materials: _____

_____

_____

_____

_____

_____

_____

Cost: _____

Notes: _____

_____

_____

_____

Name of Project: _____

Who's Doing It: _____

Tools & Materials: _____

_____

_____

_____

_____

_____

_____

Cost: _____

Notes: _____

_____

_____

_____

DIY Projects

Name of Project: _____

Who's Doing It: _____

Tools & Materials: _____

_____

_____

_____

_____

_____

Cost: _____

Notes: _____

_____

_____

_____

Name of Project: _____

Who's Doing It: _____

Tools & Materials: _____

_____

_____

_____

_____

_____

Cost: _____

Notes: _____

_____

_____

_____

DIY Projects

Name of Project: _____

Who's Doing It: _____

Tools & Materials: _____

_____

_____

_____

_____

_____

Cost: _____

Notes: _____

_____

_____

_____

Name of Project: _____

Who's Doing It: _____

Tools & Materials: _____

_____

_____

_____

_____

_____

Cost: _____

Notes: _____

_____

_____

_____

Wedding Day Timeline

Tips for writing your timeline:
- Start with the times that are set in stone - the ceremony start time and the reception start time. Then work backwards from there.
- If you've got a lot of rentals and deliveries arriving, you can even start your timeline the day before.

- Share your timeline with everyone whose name appears on the page. For example, if you want your parents to be in portraits, let them know ahead of time exactly when you'll all be meeting the photographer.
- In the week before your wedding, call all the vendors listed on your timeline and confirm their arrival times.

Time	Description	Person
9:00	Wake up!	Bride & Groom
11:00	Hair & Makeup	Bride
12:00	Wedding Party Arrives	Wedding Party
	Mimosas and Lunch	
2:00	Photographer arrives - put on dress	Bride
	First Look Photos	Bride & Groom
3:30	Formal Portraits	Bride, Groom, Parents
4:30	Guests Arrive	
5:00	Ceremony	
6:00	Reception Begins	

Time	Description	Person

Time	Description	Person

Time	Description	Person

Time	Description	Person

Vendor Contact List

Company Name: _____

Service Provided: _____

Contact Name: _____

Contact Number: _____

Email: _____

Address: _____

Company Name: _____

Service Provided: _____

Contact Name: _____

Contact Number: _____

Email: _____

Address: _____

Company Name: _____

Service Provided: _____

Contact Name: _____

Contact Number: _____

Email: _____

Address: _____

Company Name: _____

Service Provided: _____

Contact Name: _____

Contact Number: _____

Email: _____

Address: _____

Company Name: _____

Service Provided: _____

Contact Name: _____

Contact Number: _____

Email: _____

Address: _____

Company Name: _____

Service Provided: _____

Contact Name: _____

Contact Number: _____

Email: _____

Address: _____

Company Name: _____

Service Provided: _____

Contact Name: _____

Contact Number: _____

Email: _____

Address: _____

Company Name: _____

Service Provided: _____

Contact Name: _____

Contact Number: _____

Email: _____

Address: _____

Company Name: _____

Service Provided: _____

Contact Name: _____

Contact Number: _____

Email: _____

Address: _____

Company Name: _____

Service Provided: _____

Contact Name: _____

Contact Number: _____

Email: _____

Address: _____

Company Name: _____

Service Provided: _____

Contact Name: _____

Contact Number: _____

Email: _____

Address: _____

Company Name: _____

Service Provided: _____

Contact Name: _____

Contact Number: _____

Email: _____

Address: _____

Company Name: _____

Service Provided: _____

Contact Name: _____

Contact Number: _____

Email: _____

Address: _____

Company Name: _____

Service Provided: _____

Contact Name: _____

Contact Number: _____

Email: _____

Address: _____

Company Name: _____

Service Provided: _____

Contact Name: _____

Contact Number: _____

Email: _____

Address: _____

Company Name: _____

Service Provided: _____

Contact Name: _____

Contact Number: _____

Email: _____

Address: _____

Month of: _____

Sunday	Monday	Tuesday	Wednesday

Thursday	Friday	Saturday	Notes:
			_____
			_____
			_____
			_____
			_____
			_____
			_____
			_____
			_____
			_____
			_____
			_____
			_____
			_____
			_____
			_____
			_____
			_____
			_____
			_____

Month of: _____

Sunday	Monday	Tuesday	Wednesday

Thursday	Friday	Saturday	Notes:
			_____
			_____
			_____
			_____
			_____
			_____
			_____
			_____
			_____
			_____
			_____
			_____
			_____
			_____
			_____
			_____
			_____
			_____
			_____
			_____
			_____
			_____

Month of: _____

Sunday	Monday	Tuesday	Wednesday

Thursday	Friday	Saturday	Notes:
			_____
			_____
			_____
			_____
			_____
			_____
			_____
			_____
			_____
			_____
			_____
			_____
			_____
			_____
			_____
			_____
			_____
			_____
			_____
			_____
			_____
			_____

Month of: _____

Sunday	Monday	Tuesday	Wednesday

Thursday	Friday	Saturday	Notes:
			_____
			_____
			_____
			_____
			_____
			_____
			_____
			_____
			_____
			_____
			_____
			_____
			_____
			_____
			_____
			_____
			_____
			_____
			_____
			_____
			_____

Month of: _____

Sunday	Monday	Tuesday	Wednesday

Thursday	Friday	Saturday	Notes:
			_____
			_____
			_____
			_____
			_____
			_____
			_____
			_____
			_____
			_____
			_____
			_____
			_____
			_____
			_____
			_____
			_____
			_____
			_____
			_____
			_____

Month of: _____

Sunday	Monday	Tuesday	Wednesday

Thursday	Friday	Saturday	Notes:
			_____
			_____
			_____
			_____
			_____
			_____
			_____
			_____
			_____
			_____
			_____
			_____
			_____
			_____
			_____
			_____
			_____
			_____
			_____
			_____

Month of: _____

Sunday	Monday	Tuesday	Wednesday

Thursday	Friday	Saturday	Notes:
			_____
			_____
			_____
			_____
			_____
			_____
			_____
			_____
			_____
			_____
			_____
			_____
			_____
			_____
			_____
			_____
			_____
			_____
			_____
			_____

Month of: _____

Sunday	Monday	Tuesday	Wednesday

Thursday	Friday	Saturday	Notes:
			_____
			_____
			_____
			_____
			_____
			_____
			_____
			_____
			_____
			_____
			_____
			_____
			_____
			_____
			_____
			_____
			_____
			_____
			_____
			_____

Month of: _____

Sunday	Monday	Tuesday	Wednesday

Thursday	Friday	Saturday	Notes:
			_____
			_____
			_____
			_____
			_____
			_____
			_____
			_____
			_____
			_____
			_____
			_____
			_____
			_____
			_____
			_____
			_____
			_____
			_____
			_____

Month of: _____

Sunday	Monday	Tuesday	Wednesday

Thursday	Friday	Saturday	Notes:
			_____
			_____
			_____
			_____
			_____
			_____
			_____
			_____
			_____
			_____
			_____
			_____
			_____
			_____
			_____
			_____
			_____
			_____
			_____
			_____
			_____
			_____
			_____

Month of: _____

Sunday	Monday	Tuesday	Wednesday

Thursday	Friday	Saturday	Notes:
			_____
			_____
			_____
			_____
			_____
			_____
			_____
			_____
			_____
			_____
			_____
			_____
			_____
			_____
			_____
			_____
			_____
			_____
			_____
			_____

Month of: _____

Sunday	Monday	Tuesday	Wednesday

Thursday	Friday	Saturday	Notes:
			_____
			_____
			_____
			_____
			_____
			_____
			_____
			_____
			_____
			_____
			_____
			_____
			_____
			_____
			_____
			_____
			_____
			_____
			_____

About the Author

**You don't need to be a pro to plan a great wedding.
You just need the right information.**

Hi, I'm Colleen and I'm a wedding planner. If you're on a budget, you're probably not going to hire a wedding planner. But that doesn't mean you don't deserve a great wedding!

It's not that hard to plan one, as long as you've got the right information. I started writing wedding planners as a way to share that information with couples who want to do their own planning. I try to pack my books with everything you need to plan your wedding - from hiring pros to DIY. And I include tons of money saving tips along the way.

I hope you enjoyed reading The Backyard Wedding Planner.

.

If the book was useful to you, I'd love it if you left a review. An Amazon review will help other couples find the book and use it to figure out their own weddings.

Thanks for reading!

**Leave a Review:
amazon.com/author/colleenmccarthy**

Made in the USA
Las Vegas, NV
04 June 2021